Eleanor

Story and pictures by
BARBARA COONEY

VIKING

From the beginning the baby was a disappointment to her mother. She was born red and wrinkled, an ugly little thing. And she was not a boy.

Three months later they dressed her in frills and lace when the Reverend Satterlee came to the house on East 38th Street to christen her Anna Eleanor. Uncle Ted was the godfather; Aunt Tissie and Cousin Susie were the godmothers. The beautiful christening dress did not help matters much. But Eleanor's father called her "a miracle from heaven."

Although she seldom saw him, Eleanor adored her brave and handsome tiger-hunting, polo-playing father. He called her his "little Nell," throwing her high in the air, catching her amid squeals and hugs and kisses. Sometimes in her solemn way she danced for him. Eleanor felt he was the only person in the world who really cared for her.

When Eleanor was two and a half she sailed for Europe with her family on the S.S. *Britannic*. Father was not well. A change of scene, they said, might be what he needed. But the first day out, in a thick fog, the *Britannic* was rammed by another steamer. Eleanor, screaming, was dropped from the deck high above into the arms of Father in the pitching lifeboat below. From that day forward she was terrified of the ocean, and of heights as well.

Eleanor was left behind for the summer with Great-Aunt Gracie when Father and Mother sailed again.

At home most of Eleanor's waking hours were spent alone with her nanny, who spoke to Eleanor only in French.

When she and Nanny went to the park, the nannies would gather together to gossip. But while the other children played happily, Eleanor clung close to Nanny's skirts. Strange children frightened her.

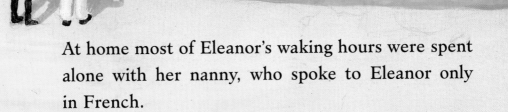

Both Father and Mother lived busy lives: fox-hunting, sailing, going to polo matches, the opera, dinners, and balls. Eleanor loved to watch her mother dressing for parties. Softly she would stroke the velvet of her mother's gown. Oh, how very beautiful her mother was! But Eleanor was not. She knew it. And, sadly, her mother knew it too.

One afternoon, put into a clean, starched dress, Eleanor was sent down to the parlor where Mother was entertaining. There, in the doorway, awkwardly biting her nails, she stood anxiously waiting to be asked in.

"Don't just stand there, Granny," said Mother to the solemn child. "Come in, please. I call her 'Granny,'" Mother said, turning to her guest, "because she is so funny and old-fashioned looking."

Eleanor wanted to sink through the floor in shame.

Not everyone lived in luxury Eleanor soon found out. When she was six she went with her father to help serve Thanksgiving dinner at a lodging house for poor newsboys. Some of these ragged street children lived in dilapidated shacks on vacant lots, but most had no homes at all and slept in boxes or under stairways or on top of steam gratings huddled together for warmth.

Once she went with Uncle Vallie to trim a Christmas tree in "Hell's Kitchen," one of the saddest and poorest sections of New York City. And, with Aunt Pussie and Aunt Maude, she sang for the homeless men at the Bowery Mission.

These expeditions she never forgot.

Eventually there were two little brothers, Ellie and Brudie. They were so much younger than Eleanor that she sat lonely and apart at the end of the day when Mother read to them by the fire.

Soon after the younger brother was born Father left home. His wild ways had failed to suit the family. But nobody explained anything to Eleanor.

Mother died of diphtheria when Eleanor was eight. Eleanor and the little brothers, alone now, moved to the big house on West 37th Street, where Grandma Hall lived with her children Aunt Pussie, Aunt Maude, Uncle Vallie, and Uncle Eddie. That same winter Ellie died too.

One spring day Father unexpectedly reappeared.
Eleanor found him sitting in a big chair in the dim
library. He was dressed all in black and looking
very sad. He gathered Eleanor in his arms and
they comforted each other. Someday, they planned,
the two of them would have a life together.

Father's visits always brought Eleanor rushing down the stairs, sliding down the banisters in her hurry. One day he called for her in a very high dogcart. While they were driving proudly up Madison Avenue on the way to Central Park, Mohawk, the horse, frightened by a streetcar, shied. Father's hat flew off. "You weren't afraid, little Nell?" her father asked.

"No," said little Nell.

But she was shaking inside.

Another day Eleanor went walking with her father and three of his fox terriers. Father left Eleanor with the dogs to wait at the door of the Knickerbocker Club. When six hours later he had failed to return, the doorman took Eleanor and the little dogs home.

Because Father forgave Eleanor for her faults Eleanor forgave his. He was the center of her world. And she never doubted that she stood first in his heart.

Father sent Eleanor many loving letters. "You must be truthful, loyal, brave, well-educated," he wrote, "to prepare for the wonderful day when we will fare forth together." They never did fare forth together, however, because when Eleanor was nine Father was killed in a fall. Nevertheless he lived on in Eleanor's dreams. She kept his letters all her life.

Now Eleanor was truly an orphan. In the winters she and Brudie lived in Grandma Hall's house, where Madeleine the governess scolded Eleanor and angrily pulled her hair when she combed it. It was a gloomy, silent house. The aunts and uncles, so much older and busy with their own affairs, were seldom home. Eleanor studied hard; she desperately wanted approval. But she still remained an outsider. Her dresses were shapeless and hung straight from her shoulders; her skirts were too short. From November to May she wore long flannel underwear. Black stockings and high button shoes completed the picture. Other girls called her a "grind."

Auntie Corinne's daughter, Corinny, was sometimes sent to have dinner with Eleanor. Corinny never wanted to go. The house was so grim, and they ate their meals in silence.

When Corinny left, she would turn and wave to the girl in the window. Then, without looking back, with a skip, she was off. Eleanor waved until Corinny was out of sight.

Summertimes were happier, despite the long black stockings. Eleanor, along with her Aunt Pussie and Aunt Maude and the uncles, went up the Hudson River to Tivoli, where Grandma Hall's house "Oak Terrace" stood on a high bluff overlooking the river. It was a high-ceilinged, drafty house lit by kerosene lamps. Every morning Eleanor and Grandma Hall went down into the deep cellar where sugar, flour, and potatoes were stored in barrels. There her grandmother would measure out exactly what the cook would need, and Eleanor would deliver it to the kitchen.

In the big old-fashioned laundry under the eye of Mrs. Overhalse, the laundress, Eleanor turned the clothes wringer and learned to iron. There was much to wash and iron. For every dress her aunts wore there were at least three petticoats.

Chores over, there were games of "I Spy," croquet, and lawn tennis, and picnics with the uncles and aunts. Eleanor learned to jump her pony, Captain. Sometimes she fished for tadpoles with her little brother, Brudie. But often she was alone with her daydreams.

On rainy days Eleanor curled up with a book. There were many books to read in Grandma Hall's library. Eleanor specialized in ones about orphans and outcasts. She thought about people less fortunate—about the newsboys and the people of Hell's Kitchen and the Bowery Mission.

On pleasant summer mornings she and Aunt Pussie sometimes got up before dawn, stole into the pantry for bread and butter, then walked through misty woods down to the river. There they climbed into a rowboat to row to the town of Tivoli, pick up the mail, and row back in time for breakfast.

Sometimes Eleanor went out to Oyster Bay on Long Island to visit Uncle Ted and Aunt Edith and the six cousins. Eleanor loved to play with golden-haired Alice, just her own age. But Alice teased Eleanor unmercifully. "She is too serious for me," said Alice. Always Eleanor was a little afraid of her.

Uncle Ted, however, loved his niece. "Eleanor, my darling Eleanor," he greeted her when she came to visit, and crushed her to his chest in such a bear hug that her buttons popped off.

Eleanor had trouble keeping up with Uncle Ted and the cousins—their wild fun, the roughhousing and crazy games of hide-and-seek, the jumping in hay mows and walking on stilts. When Uncle Ted told Eleanor to jump off the dock, she did. She sank like a rock and came up panicky and spluttering. Although she had never learned to swim, Eleanor had wished to be brave; her father and his brother, Uncle Ted, had never appreciated cowards.

Every Christmas Eleanor went with her grandmother to trim a Christmas tree for the babies in the hospital.

And every year Aunt Corinne gave a Christmas party. When Eleanor was fourteen she was allowed to attend. The other girls came to the party dressed like young ladies, in long dresses. But Eleanor was still dressed like a little girl, with blue bows on each shoulder and a skirt above her knees.

Cousin Alice danced merrily by while Eleanor stood against the wall in misery.

"Poor little soul," said Aunt Edith, "she is very plain. But the ugly duckling may turn out to be a swan."

One day, when Eleanor was just turning fifteen, Grandma Hall made an announcement: "Your mother wanted you to go to boarding school in Europe," she said, "and I have decided to send you."

She wrote to Mademoiselle Souvestre, the remarkable headmistress of Allenswood, a school near London.

"Eleanor is a good girl but sadly unattractive and full of fears. Sometimes she is afraid to tell the truth and has headaches and sleepless nights. . . ." She asked Mlle. Souvestre to admit Eleanor to the school. The letter was a challenge to the headmistress.

The next year Eleanor arrived at Allenswood. Her father's letters, tied up with ribbon, came with her. This was to be a new beginning. Behind her she left her old life and the people who pitied her for her gawkiness and for being an orphan, who teased her for being so prim. Tall and slim in her ill-fitting clothes, she stood before the little headmistress. Mlle. Souvestre, looking into Eleanor's serious blue eyes, realized that she could give a great deal to this sad young girl.

At dinner that night Eleanor shone. Allenswood had many rules. One important one was that only French was to be spoken. While the other girls sat fearful and tongue-tied, Eleanor chatted easily and happily with Mlle. Souvestre. Her old nanny had taught her well.

Life at Allenswood, strict as it was, was far from dull. Eleanor's eagerness to learn and to work pleased the teachers and the little headmistress. Among the girls, Eleanor made many friends. She was especially kind to the lonely girls far from home. Everyone called her "Totty" now. She had never felt so admired and loved before. The younger girls brought her little presents and nosegays. In her Allenswood uniform among the other girls, she stood tall and proud. She had never been happier.

The center of Eleanor's life was Mlle. Souvestre, who inspired her to think for herself, to ask questions, to be passionately committed to life and the lives of others. Mlle. was an exciting person, bursting with energy and ideas and opinions. One of her opinions was that Eleanor's clothes were, well . . . *terrible*. And she encouraged Eleanor to have made in Paris a beautiful long dark red dress. Eleanor wore it on Sundays and for everyday evening dress. Eleanor never loved a dress more.

Eleanor was Mlle. Souvestre's favorite of favorites; yet no girl begrudged her this role. She became Mlle.'s traveling companion on many holidays in Europe. Eleanor did all the packing and unpacking, made all the arrangements, figured out train schedules, bought the tickets, and arranged for cabs and porters.

They stayed in little out-of-the-way places, spoke the local language, ate the local food. At a whim, Mlle. would change plans, decide to get off a train unexpectedly to, perhaps, walk along a beach under the stars.

Mlle. Souvestre had opened the world to Eleanor.

After three happy years at Allenswood, Eleanor returned home poised and confident, brave, loyal, and true.

"Elinor has had the most admirable influence on the school and gained the affection of many, the respect of all . . ." wrote Mlle. Souvestre on Eleanor's final report card. "I feel I lose a dear friend in her."

Mlle. Souvestre had prepared Eleanor for the noble future that Father had so wanted for her.

Neither Father nor Mlle. Souvestre lived to see the remarkable woman that Eleanor would become.

When many years later she entered the White House as First Lady of the land, Eleanor carried with her Father's letters.

Mlle. Souvestre's portrait remained with her always.

AFTERWORD

Eventually Eleanor became First Lady of the United States. Her husband, Franklin Delano Roosevelt, was elected president four times, in 1932, 1936, 1940, and 1944. He and Eleanor lived in the White House with their five children, four boys and one girl.

All her life, Eleanor championed the poor and the disadvantaged. Because of her concern for social betterment, she worked with women's organizations, youth movements, and consumer-protection groups. She fought to guarantee the rights of minorities, to reduce unemployment, and to improve housing conditions. Eleanor Roosevelt was a fearless advocate of human rights, traveling all over the world, first as her husband's ambassador and, after his death, as the American delegate to the United Nations, which she helped to establish. Her intelligence and compassion and her dedication to the cause of human welfare were recognized and honored everywhere.

When Eleanor died, her friend Adlai Stevenson said of her: "She would rather light candles than curse the darkness."

For two friends: for Regina and Nonnie,

with love from Barbara

ACKNOWLEDGMENTS
The author gratefully acknowledges: William A. Farnsworth Library and Museum, Rockland, Maine; Stephen S. Garmey, vicar, Calvary Church, New York; Norman H. Morse, Portland, Maine; Library of the Boston Athenaeum; Portland (Maine) Public Library; The Metropolitan Museum of Art, New York City; Museum of the City of New York; The New-York Historical Society; Franklin D. Roosevelt Library and Museum, Hyde Park, New York; John Bradley, Knickerbocker Club archivist, New York City; Mary Howell, historian, Livingston, New York; Archives of Sagamore Hill, National Historic Site, Oyster Bay, New York; James Rivington Pyne, Waldoboro, Maine

VIKING
Published by the Penguin Group
Penguin Books USA Inc., 375 Hudson Street, New York, New York 10014, U.S.A.
Penguin Books Ltd, 27 Wrights Lane, London W8 5TZ, England
Penguin Books Australia Ltd, Ringwood, Victoria, Australia
Penguin Books Canada Ltd, 10 Alcorn Avenue, Toronto, Ontario, Canada M4V 3B2
Penguin Books (N.Z.) Ltd, 182–190 Wairau Road, Auckland 10, New Zealand

Penguin Books Ltd, Registered Offices: Harmondsworth, Middlesex, England

First published in 1996 by Viking, a division of Penguin Books USA Inc.

1 3 5 7 9 10 8 6 4 2

Copyright © Barbara Cooney, 1996
All rights reserved

LIBRARY OF CONGRESS CATALOGING-IN-PUBLICATION DATA
Cooney, Barbara.
Eleanor / by Barbara Cooney.   p.   cm.
Summary : Presents the childhood of Eleanor Roosevelt, who married a president
of the United States and became known as a great humanitarian.
ISBN 0-670-86159-6 (hardcover)
1. Roosevelt, Eleanor, 1884–1962—Childhood and youth—Juvenile literature.
2.Presidents' spouses—United States—Biography—Juvenile literature.
[1. Roosevelt, Eleanor, 1884–1962—Childhood and youth.   2. First ladies.]   I. Title.
E807.1.R48C67   1996   973.917092—dc20   [B]   96-7723 CIP AC

Printed in U.S.A.   Set in Minister